INSIDE SPECIAL FORCES™

BLACK OPS
AND OTHER SPECIAL
MISSIONS OF THE
U.S. ARMY
GREEN
BERETS

Therese Shea

rosen publishing's
rosen central®

New York

Published in 2013 by The Rosen Publishing Group, Inc.
29 East 21st Street, New York, NY 10010

Library of Congress Cataloging-in-Publication Data

Shea, Therese.
Black ops and other special missions of the U.S. Army Green Berets/Therese Shea.—1st ed.
    p. cm.—(Inside special forces)
Includes bibliographical references and index.
ISBN 978-1-4488-8381-3 (library binding)—
ISBN 978-1-4488-8387-5 (pbk.)—
ISBN 978-1-4488-8388-2 (6-pack)
1. United States. Army. Special Forces—Juvenile literature. 2. Special operations (Military science)—United States—History—Juvenile literature. 3. Special forces (Military science)—Juvenile literature. I. Title.
UA34.S64S52 2012
356'.16740973—dc23

2012017970

Manufactured in the United States of America

CPSIA Compliance Information: Batch #W13YA: For further information, contact Rosen Publishing, New York, New York, at 1-800-237-9932.

CONTENTS

INTRODUCTION

To the American public, the Army Special Forces are better known as the Green Berets. The nickname is derived from their striking headgear. This elite group stands out from other military forces because of their unique five-part mission: direct action, special reconnaissance, counterterrorism, foreign internal defense, and unconventional warfare.

For the Green Berets, direct action means capturing or destroying weapons, equipment, and personnel. These are usually "quick-strikes," meaning a unit's goals are achieved in a short period of time before the enemy can gather counterforces. Direct-action missions include detaining a terrorist or rescuing kidnapped Americans.

Special reconnaissance involves traveling undetected behind enemy lines for information. Intelligence-gathering units watch enemy camps, record types and amounts of equipment and firepower, and monitor other kinds of vital information. Intelligence may lead to a successful strike, canceling an attack, and saving civilian lives.

Following the terrorist attacks of September 11, 2001, counterterrorism is prominent among Special Forces' assignments. Not only do the Green Berets directly fight terrorists, they also train allied nations' forces to combat existing groups, such as Al Qaeda, and to stifle newly forming insurgencies. Part of this fight is cutting off weapon supplies and money to enemy organizations.

Counterterrorism is tied to the Special Forces' mission to build foreign internal defenses so that nations can protect themselves against enemies within or outside their borders. Special Forces' tactics help allied nations prevent wars. This, in turn, keeps the United States from having to deploy a large army for a full-scale conflict. Foreign internal defense extends to nations fighting illegal drug trafficking.

The last part of the mission of the Special Forces is "unconventional warfare." Conventional warfare concerns regular military forces, such as the army's infantry. Unconventional warfare means "fighting"

An Army Special Forces officer salutes at a ceremony honoring President John F. Kennedy in 2011. Kennedy was instrumental in the acceptance and growth of the Green Berets in the U.S. military.

the enemy by training forces in enemy territory. Also called guerilla warfare, these missions can last for months or years. Green Berets build relationships and armies with native tribes, minorities, and other groups suffering under a ruling power.

The motto of the Special Forces—*De oppresso liber*, or "To free the oppressed"—indicates an emphasis on working with the disenfranchised. Green Berets teach people of varying backgrounds to work together to weaken a common enemy. To win trust and respect, Green Berets are skilled in diplomacy.

The Special Forces' official Web site asserts this declaration: "Your most powerful weapon is your mind." Unlike most members of the military, Special Forces soldiers are often out of contact with their commanding officers. They make decisions that can greatly impact the direction of warfare in a country. They live among the people they are helping and among the enemies, too. They seamlessly blend in and then just disappear. Courage is needed, but so is a keen intelligence.

Because of their work behind enemy lines, many Special Forces' operations are at least partly classified. Some missions are never publicly acknowledged. Covert missions such as these are called black operations, or black ops. This book describes some of the remarkable missions—both classified and celebrated—of these elite American soldiers throughout their history.

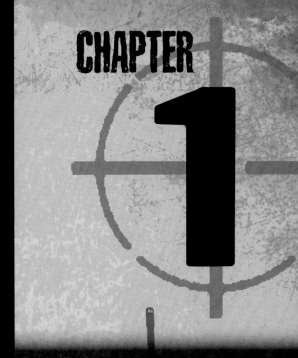

BUILDING AN *ELITE* FORCE

The Special Forces date back to 1952 officially, but their origins are traced to World War II in the Office of Strategic Services (OSS). The OSS's purpose was to gather intelligence and conduct missions behind enemy lines. Small teams undertook the "Jedburgh Project," dropping into France, Belgium, and Holland to train resistance groups and carry out guerilla operations against the Germans. The OSS operated in Asia, too. In Burma (now Myanmar), an OSS team trained 11,000 Kachin tribesmen, a force that eventually killed 10,000 Japanese with a loss of just 206 of their own. The OSS disbanded after the war.

FULFILLING A NEED

U.S. Colonel Aaron Bank had been an OSS officer and member of a three-man Jedburgh unit involved in sabotage and other missions. Bank felt that the American army could benefit from similar covert teams. Their specialized skills could prevent another large-scale war and modernize the U.S. military. He also believed certain conflicts of that time, such as those with the Communist Soviet Union, could be better managed with small unconventional forces, rather than large operations. (This was also a less expensive option.) While the Army Rangers were a special operations force known for fast-moving, direct-attack missions, Bank's force might spend months or years in enemy territory without support.

It was a new way of thinking. Bank, Brigadier General Robert McClure (known for psychological warfare operations in World War II), Colonel Russell Volckmann (known for guerilla resistance in the Philippines), and several others pooled their experiences to create the Army Special Forces.

On June 20, 1952, the 10th Special Forces Group was established, with Bank as its commander. It initially consisted of seven enlisted men, one warrant officer, and Bank. However, its numbers swelled, and the group split in two the following year, creating the 77th Special Forces Group. Fort Bragg in North Carolina housed the 77th, while the 10th's base was located in West Germany.

In 1961, another vital contributor to Special Forces policy was appointed to head the training center, the U.S. Army Warfare Center/School for Special Warfare at Fort Bragg. Lieutenant General William Yarborough encouraged the institution to

THE ORIGIN OF THE GREEN BERET

William Yarborough orchestrated the visit of President John F. Kennedy to Fort Bragg on October 12, 1961. Kennedy was interested in counterinsurgency efforts and realized that this part of the army could carry out such missions. On that day, the Special Forces soldiers were wearing their unofficial headgear, the green beret. They wore them during certain exercises to distinguish themselves from regular

soldiers. According to the John F. Kennedy Presidential Library and Museum Web site, after viewing an impressive demonstration of their skills, the president asked Yarborough, "How do you like the green beret?" General Yarborough replied, "They're fine, Sir. We've wanted them a long time." Soon after, President Kennedy authorized the green beret as the official headgear for U.S. Army

Lieutenant General William Yarborough *(right)* is pictured speaking to President John F. Kennedy at Fort Bragg in 1961. When the president gave his blessing to the green beret headgear, he helped the Special Forces set themselves apart physically from other army forces.

Special Forces, and the public embraced Green Berets as a nickname for the force. When Kennedy was assassinated, Special Forces were asked to be part of his funeral's honor guard. Today, a wreath from the Green Berets is still placed on Kennedy's grave to honor his role in the evolution of this military force.

become more like a university, inviting speakers on a variety of subjects. Perhaps most important to his legacy, Yarborough impressed upon the Special Forces the importance of civil affairs in their work, particularly winning the hearts and minds of the people of a nation. This idea was borrowed from Mao Zedong, the Communist revolutionary, who used it to rise to power in China. Eventually, this principle was absorbed into the Green Berets' mission.

TRAINING TODAY

The multipart mission of the Special Forces demands its soldiers have many skills. Over the years, Green Beret training evolved into its current level of intensity. Green Berets go through the same training as enlisted soldiers. This includes ten challenging weeks of basic combat training. After that awaits the Special Operations Preparation Course (SOPC) at Fort Bragg, North Carolina: thirty days of physical training with an emphasis on land navigation, a vital ability for a Green Beret dropped into enemy territory. Next is

the Special Forces Assessment and Selection (SFAS) at Camp Mackall in North Carolina. Over twenty-four days, a candidate's intelligence, agility, and resourcefulness is tested, as well as his ability to cope with stress. Activities include physical tests—swimming, running, and marching—and mental and psychological tests, such as unit tactics and orienteering.

This Special Forces soldier competes with others to earn a position as a trainer of Green Beret recruits. He ties logs together, which he will carry through the deserts of Afghanistan as a test of strength and endurance.

Following the SFAS is the Special Forces Qualification Course (SFQC), which consists of five phases. The first phase, individual skill, is thirteen weeks of land navigation, live-round weapons training, small-unit tactics, language acquisition, and survival skills. The next is MOS (Military Occupation Specialty) training. Over fifteen weeks, the candidate learns an occupation based on his background, interest, and talent. He also continues to focus on language skills and tactics.

Special Forces Qualification Course students communicate with team members during training in North Carolina. The environments in which students train can be harsh and demanding.

The four-week phase that follows is collective training during which candidates focus on the Special Forces' mission and organization. They study unconventional warfare, direct action, and airborne operations. They deploy to Uwharrie National Forest in North Carolina for an exercise in which their MOS and overall skills are evaluated. In the next language-training phase, the candidate is expected to perfect his proficiency in at least one foreign language over fourteen weeks. Common languages are Arabic, Spanish, Chinese, and Russian.

The SERE Course is the final phase of the SFQC. SERE stands for survival, evasion, resistance, and escape. Candidates live nineteen days as if they were prisoners of war (POWs). The camp is based on real-life POW camps. Military personnel convincingly act as jailers and interrogators. The situation feels authentic and stressful to the candidate. How stressful? Under conditions of sleep deprivation and semi-starvation, much like real POW camps, candidates may lose 22 pounds (10 kilograms) in three days according to a *Newsweek* article.

The underlying idea is that extreme pressure will acclimate the soldier to other high-strain situations so that he will be able to think clearly in a crisis. In a stress study, Special Forces soldiers recovered from high stress levels more quickly than other soldiers.

Once completing SERE, the candidate qualifies to become a Special Forces soldier. He may receive live environment training in another country to become fully immersed in a new culture as well.

Special Forces education is still changing according to times and needs. The army now uses simulation software, called adaptive thinking and leadership game training, to test mental agility and cultural sensitivity, key components in Special Forces' work in foreign nations. How difficult is it to complete all of these courses in order to become a Green Beret? According to a *USA Today* article, three out of four candidates do not complete the training.

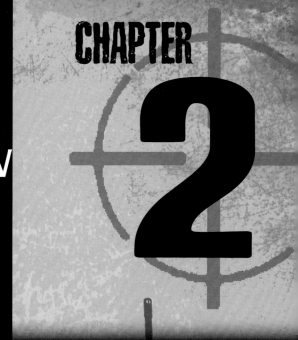

CHAPTER 2

A-TEAMS AND ORGANIZATION

Green Berets work in small units, usually of twelve men. Each team is called an Operational Detachment Alpha (ODA), and informally the Alpha Team or A-Team. Though detachments change with the needs of each assignment, an ODA often has two sergeants of each of the following military occupational specialties: weapons, engineering, medical, and communications. There is also an intelligence sergeant and an operations sergeant. Members of the ODA are cross-trained to have some knowledge of all these occupational specialties. Teams can split in two when needed.

MEMBERS OF THE TEAM

A Special Forces weapons sergeant specializes in light and heavy weaponry. He not only learns how to operate U.S. weapons but also those of allies and enemies. He may train and equip friendly forces for raids and carry out operations to destroy enemy weapons. Weapons sergeants are usually required to be divers, paratroopers, and endurance runners as well. Forty-three weeks of training and exercises condition these soldiers to use all kinds of weapons in the most stressful circumstances.

The Special Forces engineer sergeant is a jack-of-all-trades, including demolition, surveying, and construction. These soldiers interpret maps, charts, and photos and navigate the team through enemy territory. They carry out missions to sabotage enemy bridges, roads, and fuel supplies. They complete additional training similar to weapons sergeants.

Special Forces medical sergeants are the first responders when their detachment or allies need medical attention. Trauma and emergency medicine are their primary concerns, but they also have knowledge of dentistry, water quality, and even animal care. Their sixty-week training conditions them in swimming, parachuting, and survival like other members of the ODA.

The Special Forces communications sergeant is an expert in communications equipment and codes transmitted by satellite or other means. He organizes, trains, and advises the setup and use of communications equipment. He reports intelligence back to base and may work to dismantle the communications of enemy targets. He, too, completes a sixty-week course in preparation for his duties.

A commanding officer—a captain—and assistant commander—a warrant officer—complete the ODA.

The Special Forces officers are the team leaders of the ODA. They organize each mission, making sure the team has the knowledge and gear needed to complete the objective and is ready to alter the mission when needed. They are also the commanding officers of guerrilla and insurgent forces and advisers to foreign leaders and officials.

WEAPONS, GEAR, AND VEHICLES

Special Forces are called upon to operate in almost every region of the world, and they employ different types of weapons, equipment, and vehicles to help them accomplish their missions. Firearms include pistols, rifles, machine pistols, machine guns, shotguns, grenades, rocket launchers, and mortars.

The M-4 carbine is a lightweight rifle customized with different scopes depending on the needs of the mission. The Green Berets also use the M-9 pistol. A laser pointer may be attached to this semiautomatic firearm, increasing its accuracy. For an armored target, such as a tank, Special Forces may use the Javelin missile system. The Javelin locks on to the heat created by the target vehicle. Once launched, the shooter can either load and fire another missile or move to a new position. Remarkably, this powerful weapon is light enough to be fired by a single soldier, though carried by two.

Green Berets are often inserted into their area of operation by air. Special Forces insertion helicopters include the MH-60 Pave Hawk. It may be equipped with weapons systems to use against the enemy when

The M-4 carbine firearm is equipped with a heat-seeking weapons sight *(top)* and daylight video sight *(right of barrel)*, technology added to make the weapon more precise than those of the enemy.

HALO (high-altitude, low-opening) jumping involves soldiers exiting a plane at around 25,000 feet (7,620 meters) and free-falling to 3,500 feet (1,067 m) before opening a parachute. They may descend this distance within two minutes.

necessary. The Pave Hawk is also notable for search-and-rescue operations. When a larger helicopter is needed, the Green Berets use the MH-47 Chinook. The Chinook is capable of transporting soldiers long distances and can be refueled in the air. It has a rope system that allows soldiers to rappel rapidly from a hovering helicopter to the ground.

HALO (high-altitude, low-opening) describes a special jump from an aircraft at a great height. The soldier then waits until he is close to the ground to open up his parachute. This technique makes it difficult for Special Forces to be noticed by radar. The HALO helmet allows a soldier to breathe from an oxygen supply during the jump.

Green Berets sometimes perform their missions in the water. They use kayaks and small inflatable boats to navigate waterways. They may use a rebreather to swim through rivers and streams virtually unnoticed.

In the desert, Special Forces patrols use the GMV, or ground mobility vehicle. It is a heavily armed

THE SPECIAL FORCES CREED

"I am an American Special Forces Soldier!

I will do all that my nation requires of me. I am a volunteer, knowing well the hazards of my profession.

I serve with the memory of those who have gone before me. I pledge to uphold the honor and integrity of their legacy in all that I am—in all that I do.

I am a warrior. I will teach and fight whenever and wherever my nation requires. I will strive always to excel in every art and artifice of war.

I know that I will be called upon to perform tasks in isolation, far from familiar faces and voices. With the help and guidance of my faith, I will conquer my fears and succeed.

I will keep my mind and body clean, alert and strong. I will maintain my arms and equipment in an immaculate state befitting a Special Forces Soldier, for this is my debt to those who depend upon me.

I will not fail those with whom I serve. I will not bring shame upon myself or Special Forces.

I will never leave a fallen comrade. I will never surrender though I am the last. If I am taken, I pray that I have the strength to defy my enemy.

I am a member of my Nation's chosen soldiery. I serve quietly, not seeking recognition or accolades. My goal is to succeed in my mission—and live to succeed again.

De Oppresso Liber"

Humvee. GMVs provide space for three men to carry enough ammunition, food, fuel, and weapons for a ten-day mission. LMTV (light medium tactical vehicles) "War Pigs" are supply trucks fitted with weapons systems. However, Special Forces adapt to their environment. In 2001, for instance, Green Berets rode on horseback with their allies into Afghanistan.

THE ORGANIZATION

Six ODAs and a headquarters (operational detachment B) make up a company. The ODB manages operations. Within a Special Forces company, one ODA receives special training in airborne insertion and another ODA is trained in water insertion. Both of these approaches, along with ground operations, are used to get Green Berets quickly and quietly behind enemy lines.

Three Special Forces companies, a support company, and a headquarters comprise a battalion. A battalion provides command, logistics, and analysis to deploying detachments. Three battalions, a headquarters, and support make up a Special Forces Group (SFG). There are five active-duty Green Beret groups:

- 1st SFG is stationed at Joint Base Lewis-McChord, Washington, with an area of operation (AO) of East Asia and the Pacific

- 3rd SFG is stationed at Fort Bragg, North Carolina, with an AO of sub-Saharan Africa

- 5th SFG is stationed at Fort Campbell, Kentucky, with an AO of the Middle East and Central Asia

- 7th SFG is stationed at Eglin Air Force Base, Florida, with an AO of Central and South America and the Caribbean

- 10th SFG is stationed at Fort Carson, Colorado, with an AO of Europe, North Africa, and Western Asia

Two Special Forces National Guard groups, the 19th and 20th, are headquartered in Draper, Utah, and Birmingham, Alabama, respectively, and share AOs with the 1st, 5th, and 7th.

The wreckage of a U.S. plane in Iran serves as a reminder of Operation Eagle Claw in 1980. Out of this failure came a unified command from which the Special Forces would receive many of their future missions.

SFGs may operate outside their AOs in times of need. Many are currently serving tours of duty in Afghanistan, as well as having deployments in Iraq. All U.S. Army special operations forces report to U.S. Army Special Operations Command (USASOC) headquartered in Fort Bragg, North Carolina.

SOCOM

In 1980, the United States sent a military force including Green Berets to Iran to free American hostages in a mission called Operation Eagle Claw. A series of events led to the deaths and injuries of several soldiers, the release of classified information to Iranian forces, and the cancellation of the mission. The hostages were not released until the following year.

Out of the botched assignment came the realization that a unified command, sharing resources and equipment, could better handle special operations involving more than one military branch. Congress created a joint special operations headquarters. The U.S. Special Operations Command (SOCOM) was activated in 1987 as the overseeing command of the special operations of the army, air force, navy, and marine corps. SOCOM, located at MacDill Air Force Base in Florida, has become, according to an article on NavySEALs.com, a "fifth service" of the U.S. military and has made it common for Green Berets to work alongside the air force and navy.

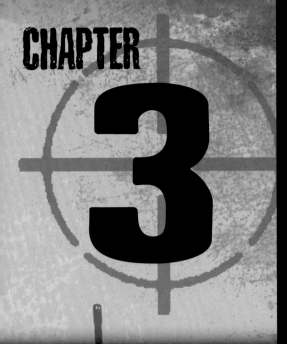

CHAPTER 3

WAR IN SOUTHEAST ASIA

During the 1950s and 1960s, Communism was a great concern of the U.S. military. The "domino theory"—the idea that if one country adopted Communist principles, then the countries around it would also fall to Communism—led the United States to send financial and military support to areas susceptible to Communist insurgencies.

The first known Special Forces missions took place in Korea at the end of 1952. These missions were classified for thirty years. We now know Green Berets assisted guerrilla forces that had fled Communist North Korea at the outset of the Korean War. These forces joined with the United Nations Partisan Forces—Korea (UNPFK) and grew to more than twenty-two thousand. They conducted raids, rescues, and attacks, and claimed to have killed sixty-nine thousand enemy soldiers. Beginning in 1953, Green Berets began training to operate in other parts of Southeast Asia, including Taiwan, Thailand, and French Indochina (now Vietnam, Cambodia, and Laos).

LAOS

Since its independence in 1954, Laos experienced an internal power struggle. In 1959, twelve U.S. Special Forces teams from the 77th Special Forces Group (now the 7th) were sent into Laos to help the French

An army unit adapts to the terrain in Thailand in the early 1960s. They readied themselves for a Pathet Lao invasion with guerrilla warfare tactics.

train the Laotian army to combat the Communist Pathet Lao forces. This mission was so covert that the Green Berets wore civilian clothes, not soldiers' uniforms, and even carried civilian identification.

When the French military left in 1960, the American Special Forces became a visible and acknowledged presence known as White Star Mobile Training Teams. Besides training Laotian soldiers, the Green Berets worked on winning the support of the Laotian people through building, providing supplies, and implementing programs to improve their lives. However, the U.S. military was forced to officially pull out of Laos in 1962 because of the Geneva Accords. However, as the North Vietnamese continued supporting the Pathet Lao, Green Berets stayed behind in a clandestine training operation with the Meo warriors of Laos.

VIETNAM

Throughout the Vietnam War, the Green Berets trained and fought alongside the people of South Vietnam against the Communist North Vietnamese Army (NVA). Vietnam was made up of many different peoples. One of the Special Forces' most successful efforts was working with the Montagnards, the name for the various minorities and tribal people living in the central highlands of Vietnam. In conjunction with the CIA, the Green Berets implemented a program called the Civilian Irregular Defense Group (CIDG).

Beginning in 1961, two Special Forces A-detachments from the 5th Special Forces Group, 1st Special Forces, began work on the Village Defense Program as part of the CIDG. These Green Berets won the trust of the Montagnards. They recruited and trained men to be a security force for their own village and network with other villages to combat the South Vietnamese Communist insurgency called the Viet Cong (VC) as well as the NVA.

With this defense established, the Green Berets focused on improving the lives of the people with sanitation projects, medicine, and other developments. The program proved so successful that villages asked to be included, expanding the U.S.-friendly territory and denying the VC and NVA the hearts and minds of these indigenous people, as well as the goods and services they could provide.

MINING THE HO CHI MINH TRAIL

North Vietnam used a complex system of mountain and jungle paths called the Ho Chi Minh Trail to bring troops and supplies into South Vietnam, Cambodia, and Laos. To disrupt their progress, Green Berets sabotaged parts of the trail. Sergeant Dennis Mack tells the tale of one operation into Cambodia to mine the trail in the book *War Stories of the Green Berets*.

Mack's team was dropped off several miles from the trail to mask their presence from the NVA. Once they got to the trail, Mack's job as the detachment engineer was to plant a mine. Just as he finished digging a hole with his knife, another member of the detachment signaled. An NVA sentry was approaching. Mack withdrew into the jungle. The sentry saw the freshly dug hole and began to walk into the jungle to investigate. The soldier did not see Mack until the Green Beret's rifle was nearly touching his face. Mack relates, "Well, I smiled at him, thinking, 'You are in big trouble now, buddy.' He smiled back. Then he backed up, got back on the road, and kept walking!"

Mack knew he could not shoot the sentry or the noise would alert other enemies. He assumed the man would tell his superior officers of what he had found. Still, Mack planted the mine and made his way back to a safe spot. Later that night, the Green Beret heard trucks moving up the road and then . . . the

Abandoned vehicles remain on a rural part of the Ho Chi Minh Trail. Though some of the paths have been covered by jungle, other routes have been paved and transformed into a major highway.

Master Sergeant Charles Hosking, Jr., served two tours of duty in Vietnam as well as served in World War II. His actions as a Special Forces soldier in Vietnam earned him the military's highest decoration—the Medal of Honor.

mine exploded. The sentry had not alerted anyone of the Americans or the mine. Mack thinks allowing the man to live might have saved the mission.

MEDAL OF HONOR ACTIONS

The 5th Special Forces Group displayed a selfless courage to their fellow Americans as well as their CIDG units. In 1967, Master Sergeant Charles Hosking, Jr., served as an adviser to a South Vietnamese battalion that had captured a Viet Cong sniper. While the prisoner was being taken back to camp, he grabbed a grenade from Hosking's belt and ran toward a group of American and Vietnamese soldiers. Hosking jumped on the sniper's back and "bear hugged" him, keeping the grenade between them. The blast killed both men instantly.

A year later, Specialist John Kedenburg headed a small reconnaissance team into enemy territory to perform counterguerilla operations. The team's mission was interrupted when they became encircled by

BLACK SOGS

During the Vietnam War, a successful—and highly classified—surveillance campaign using Special Forces soldiers was set up near the borders of Laos and Cambodia. It was called Project 404. U.S. military crossed into politically neutral Laos as civilians for short periods of time and completed missions. It was a way of working around the Geneva Accords but held great risks for the men who volunteered for these missions. Had they been captured, they would have had no rights as prisoners of war under the Geneva Convention. These "black" Studies and Operations Groups (SOGs) listened in to communications from the North Vietnamese Army, captured soldiers for intelligence, planted sensors to detect enemy movements, and performed rescues, all within a few miles of the border. At first, the U.S. Department of Defense denied these activities were taking place.

However, in 1970, SOGs led several North Vietnamese battalions into an ambush by U.S. aircraft. More than five hundred NVA were killed and about a dozen Green Berets. A few months later, the SOGs were finally acknowledged publicly by the Department of Defense but only as reconnaissance teams. The classified files were later opened by Congress.

a large North Vietnamese Army force. Under Kedenburg's command, the team broke out of the circle and moved toward territory where they could be rescued by a helicopter. With Kedenburg taking the rear to protect the fleeing group, the group reached the land site, minus a South Vietnamese soldier assumed killed. At the site, the missing soldier appeared. One soldier would not be able to leave the landing zone. Without hesitation, Kedenburg gave up his space in the helicopter. As NVA soldiers reached the site, Kedenburg's men looked down to see their leader kill six enemy soldiers before finally being overpowered.

Kedenburg and Hosking received Medals of Honor posthumously for their selfless sacrifices.

THE SON TAY MISSION

In 1970, a team of Army Special Forces soldiers and Air Force Special Operations planned an attack on a North Vietnamese prisoner-of-war camp to free U.S. soldiers being held there. Son Tay camp was deep in enemy territory, less than 30 miles (48 km) from the capital city, Hanoi. The rescue team practiced in a model of the camp.

On the night of November 20, a force including six helicopters, two support aircraft, and five attack planes took off from Thailand. A navy aircraft carrier was poised to create a diversion near the camp as well. At 2 AM, the Americans reached Son Tay, first taking out the guard towers. Another helicopter completed a planned crash landing, delivering Green Berets to the ground. Two more helicopters landed soon after. But the soldiers reported their findings: "negative items." The camp was empty of POWs. Later intelligence found that the POWs had been moved.

Though no prisoners were saved, this famous mission was considered a success for several reasons. All fifty-six soldiers returned to base—not one life had been lost. It was also an example of superior cooperative strategy among military branches. Last, American POWs would later report hearing of the attempt and said it boosted their morale. They and the North Vietnamese Army received the message: the United States would not forget their soldiers.

MIXED SUCCESS

By the time the 5th Special Forces Group left Southeast Asia in 1971, its soldiers had won sixteen of the seventeen Medals of Honor awarded to the Special Forces in Vietnam, 1 Distinguished Service Medal, 90 Distinguished Service Crosses, 814 Silver Stars, 13,234 Bronze Stars, 235 Legions of Merit, 46 Distinguished Flying Crosses, 232 Soldier's Medals, 4,891 Air Medals, 6,908 Army Commendation Medals, and 2,658 Purple Hearts.

As the CIDG program grew larger, approaching sixty thousand members, its command was changed in 1963. This resulted in removing the task of managing the guerrillas from the Special Forces' objectives. The Green Berets were thought to be better used in surveillance camps near the border of South Vietnam.

Eventually, the South Vietnamese were given control of the program. The changes in command, unfortunately, were enough for the guerrilla army to lose much of its effectiveness. The animosity and suspicion that had long existed between the Montagnards and the Vietnamese remained. The CIDG ended in 1970. Americans would later withdraw, and all of Vietnam would be enveloped by the Communist regime.

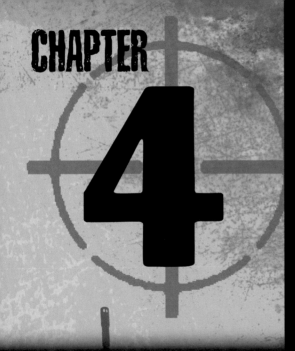

CHAPTER 4

BERETS BACK IN THE SPOTLIGHT

After the Vietnam War, the 3rd, 6th, and 8th Special Forces Groups were deactivated. By 1978, the Green Berets only consisted of the 5th, 7th, and the 10th. The U.S. military leaders, for the most part, did not see a use for their skills in peacetime. It did not help that the U.S. Army and the Special Forces had clashed in Vietnam and other areas. There were even reports of Special Forces penetrating U.S. command posts, just to reveal their weaknesses. Most members of the military high command supported conventional warfare tactics over special operations like those of the Green Berets. In an effort to stay relevant, the SPARTAN (Special Proficiency at Rugged Training and Nation-building) program was implemented in Florida, Arizona, and Montana. Among other in-nation activities, the 5th and

Edward C. Meyer served in Vietnam from 1965 to 1970. He was named a general in 1979. As chief of staff, he helped rebuild an army that had suffered during the unpopular Vietnam War.

7th Special Forces Groups worked with Native American tribes building roads and medical facilities.

General Edward C. Meyer, the Chief of Staff of the army, is credited with bringing the Special Forces back to their former glory. In 1984, Meyer activated the 1st Special Forces Group, helped develop a plan for the future of the Green Berets, and made changes to the special operations command structure. The Green Berets became a major command in 1987 with a three-star lieutenant general. This meant they had the authority to oversee their own training programs, among other powers. Also, the length of Special Forces qualification courses increased to ensure that its ranks held only the most highly skilled soldiers.

IN CENTRAL AMERICA

In the early 1980s, the Green Berets were again called to perform missions that recalled their original purpose. Terrorism, insurgencies, and unconventional threats were rising around the globe, including in Central America. Green Berets assisted several nations, including El Salvador, in building internal defenses that could stop the growth of the Communist guerrilla forces. The 7th Special Forces Group played a vital role in preparing the Honduran military to put down unrest caused by civil war in nearby Nicaragua.

A Special Forces soldier talks to a U.S. drug-control official about special military operations to control the cocaine trade in Colombia.

Green Berets assisted them in conducting counter-insurgency operations and ultimately defeating a Honduran Communist uprising.

Later in the decade, the Green Berets focused on counter-drug operations in Colombia, Venezuela, Peru, Ecuador, and Bolivia. Breaking down drug syndicates was a new kind of mission for the Green Berets, but one vital to keeping peace in many of these nations.

OPERATION JUST CAUSE

In December 1989, Special Forces from the 5th and 7th Special Forces Groups were called to support conventional army units in Operation Just Cause, an invasion of Panama to depose dictator Manuel Noriega. Task Force Black—as the Special Forces from the 7th were called—conducted reconnaissance, direct attacks, and "blocking" tactics. In one of these missions, though outnumbered, they secured a bridge at the Pacora River and engaged Panama defense forces in gunfire, preventing Panamanian reinforcements from reaching U.S. Rangers.

The Green Berets suffered no casualties throughout the short—but highly successful—operation. Following the monthlong conflict, Operation Promote Liberty commenced. The Green Berets' new mission began: to train Panama's police force, which would guide the country as it transformed into a democratic republic.

DESERT STORM

During the Gulf War against Iraq (1990–1991), Green Beret detachments provided special reconnaissance.

MOVIES, BOOKS, MUSIC, AND RADIO

The Green Berets have long captured the imagination of the public. A 1968 movie called *The Green Berets* starring John Wayne depicted Special Forces in Vietnam. It was partly based on a book of the same title by Robin Moore. Moore also coauthored the lyrics of a song with Staff Sergeant Barry Sadler called "Ballad of the Green Berets," which was first released in 1966. Despite the unpopularity of the Vietnam War, this song was a number 1 hit and increased the public's interest in the U.S. Army Special Forces. The film series following the fictional character John Rambo, played by Sylvester Stallone, is also about a Green Beret. The 1980s TV series and the 2010 movie *The A-Team* were both fictional accounts of four Army Special Forces soldiers running from the government.

Small teams were inserted into enemy territory by MH-53J helicopters called Pave Lows, designed to fly low to make detection less likely. Pave Lows dropped Special Forces behind lines to test soil to determine whether the sandy routes could carry American tanks and other heavy vehicles. The soldiers also recorded routes on camera for a better visual understanding of the environment.

Another type of intelligence-gathering mission behind enemy lines involved lengthier stays. Each soldier in a small team was equipped with about 175 pounds (79 kg) of communications gear, submachine guns, grenade launchers, and other light weapons. A helicopter "pretended" to drop the team several times in various places, in case its position was picked up by radar. After the actual drop, the Special Forces unit created a "hide site" in a sparsely populated area, essentially by digging a large hole and covering it with a tarp. From their hide site, the soldiers reported Iraqi troop movements and other intelligence. Unfortunately, many of these missions were aborted after the Green Berets' positions were discovered.

In one such mission, described in the book *Shadow Warriors*, a team of three Green Berets was discovered in a field by Bedouins, who began firing at them. Not wanting to harm civilians, the Special Forces held off the attack and called for air rescue, a risky procedure in daylight. An American F-16 fighter jet dropped bombs around the attackers in an attempt to scare them. Meanwhile, Iraqi soldiers were alerted of the Americans' presence and closed in. The Special Forces' ammunition began dwindling. They uneasily felt their grenades, knowing they could be used to take out several of the enemies and themselves as well.

Suddenly, a Special Forces Black Hawk helicopter swooped over the top of a group of Iraqis and nearly landed on the Green Berets. As the gunner in the helicopter provided cover with a shower of bullets, the Special Forces team hopped aboard. The now-battered Black Hawk arrived safely back in friendly territory.

A Special Forces airborne unit practices a medical evacuation in a Black Hawk helicopter. Black Hawks assist in air assault, evacuations, and special operations combat support.

The Green Berets took part in many search-and-rescue operations such as this in Iraq. They also instructed coalition forces. Special Forces–trained Kuwaiti and Arab military units, backed by air support, were the main force that retook Kuwait City from Iraqi occupation. They found that the Iraqi forces had already fled. The ground war halted about eleven hours after it began. The success of Operation Desert Storm, as it was called, and the essential part played by all special operations forces validated both the Green Berets' and SOCOM's purpose.

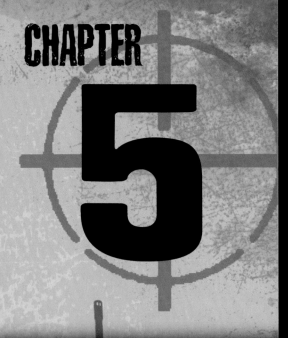

5

U.S. SPECIAL FORCES IN IRAQ AND AFGHANISTAN

In 2004, special operations commander Brigadier General Gary L. Harrell told the *New York Times* that the Iraq War was the largest use of special operations in any conflict. More than ten thousand elite soldiers participated in Operation Iraqi Freedom. The Green Berets played a key role in reconnaissance missions, as well as striving to win the "hearts and minds" of Iraqi civilians, working to make them allies in opposing the regime of Saddam Hussein. Special Forces continue to perform such assignments in Afghanistan today.

AN "ALAMO" IN IRAQ

Even before the invasion of Iraq in 2003, Army Special Forces crossed into northern Iraq to gather intelligence and train Kurdish fighters. These willing Kurds called themselves Peshmerga, which means "ready to die." A few weeks after the war began in 2003, an objective was targeted: cut off the Iraqi army from the north by capturing a strategic crossroads. This was the first major offensive to move south from Kurdish zones to territory controlled by Hussein's government. It came to be called the Battle of Debecka Pass.

Combat began with a series of B-52 air strikes. Two Special Forces teams from the 3rd and 10th Special Forces Groups—ODA 391 and ODA 392—readied

The B-52 is a long-range heavy bomber that can perform a variety of missions at altitudes up to 50,000 feet (15,240 m). Its air support aided the Army Special Forces prior to the Battle of Debecka Pass.

themselves for combat against an Iraqi rifle company of hundreds, including tanks and armored personnel carriers. The Green Berets, numbering twenty-six, worked alongside the air force and two other soldiers. They settled on a plateau above a highway. Being far outnumbered, outgunned, and outarmored, they needed distance and cover to survive.

As a four-and-a-half-hour firefight began, the small force dodged tank and mortar shells. Close hits brought heavy rains of dirt onto their heads. About eighty Peshmergas worked below to destroy a manmade wall of earth that separated the two forces. The Americans had plenty of firepower, though, including shoulder-launched Javelin anti-tank missile systems. These proved to be the key to the battle. The detachments scored seventeen hits for nineteen shots, destroying vehicles and sending their occupants scrambling for cover. This accuracy was incredible considering the missiles were fired much farther from the recommended maximum range of 1.2 miles (2,000 m). The Iraqis began to crumble under the pressure. Some were killed by their own force while trying to surrender.

By the end of the battle, no American casualties were reported. (Seventeen Kurdish soldiers and forty-five other coalition soldiers were wounded by a friendly-fire air strike.) The detachments achieved their objective, securing the crossroads, and later moved farther into enemy territory with the help of a Navy F-18 bomber jet.

Though listed as classified at first, this mission was later disclosed to honor the soldiers' actions. Special Forces Staff Sergeants Jeffrey M. Adamec and Jason D. Brown each received a Silver Star following the battle and were named "Javelin aces." Adamec told the *New York Times*: "We all made a promise. Nobody had to yell out commands. Everybody just knew. We were not going to move back from that point. We were not going to give up that ground. We called that spot 'the Alamo.'"

Kurdish Peshmergas and Army Special Forces work together in Iraq in 2003. The Iraqi Kurds had been oppressed by Saddam Hussein's regime and were eager to join the fight against him.

OPERATION CHROMIUM

After Saddam Hussein was captured and his regime toppled, the Green Berets became highly involved in training the new Iraqi forces, which would defend the country when U.S. forces left. They also collected intelligence to locate insurgents fighting the newly installed government.

On September 10, 2003, Green Berets from the 10th Special Forces Group, ODA 083, collaborated with Iraqi National Police to capture Abu Obediah, an Al Qaeda minister of defense wanted for kidnapping and murder. The mission was called Operation Chromium. During the night, the coalition force traveled by helicopter north of Baghdad in a surprise attack on an insurgent stronghold. However, the planned landing site was covered by water so that the helicopters landed closer to the compound. The noise alerted the insurgents, and heavy machine-gun fire erupted from three buildings.

Sergeant First Class Jarion Halbisengibbs, a weapons sergeant, directed the Iraqi forces into the nearest building. He and two other Green Berets—Sergeant First Class Michael Lindsay and Captain Matthew Chaney—charged into another building, killing three insurgents as they pushed on to the farthest building. Halbisengibbs tossed a grenade through the door, killing two more enemy fighters and allowing all three Green Berets inside. Chaney and Lindsay, wounded but still firing, were blown out the door by the force of a second explosion. Halbisengibbs was thrown into the corner of the room. Wearing his night-vision goggles, he kept firing despite wounds in his hand, stomach, and hip. He managed to kill six insurgents, at the same time directing Iraqi police with his radio. Eventually, all the insurgents, including Abu Obediah, were killed and their weapons seized. A hostage was rescued as well. Staff Sergeant Halbisengibbs was awarded the Distinguished Service Cross in 2009 for his tenacity in combat.

OPERATION ENDURING FREEDOM

Operation Enduring Freedom was the U.S. response in Afghanistan to the September 11, 2001, terrorist attacks. The objectives included toppling the Taliban government and breaking the Al Qaeda influence on the country. As with the Iraq War, Special Forces were sent into Afghanistan on reconnaissance missions months before conventional military forces entered the country. They also worked with Afghanistan's opposition forces, especially the Northern Alliance. The U.S.-led forces fractured the Taliban regime within months, allowing a new Afghan government to form. Special Forces remain today, training the Afghan National Army and hunting for Al Qaeda terrorists.

MILLER'S LAST MISSION

In 2008, a team of twenty-four Green Berets and Afghan soldiers led by Staff Sergeant Robert Miller of the 3rd Special Forces Group were on a night-time mission in a northwest part of Afghanistan.

Their aim was to clear a valley of insurgents who had been attacking Afghan soldiers and villages. The small force found an enemy compound and called in an air strike for assistance. After the strike, they approached the heavily damaged building.

Miller was at the front of the group when an insurgent jumped out at them. Suddenly, the whole valley lit up the night with gunfire and grenades. Miller's men—just two dozen—were caught without cover by about 150 insurgents. Miller, the only one of his group who could speak the Afghan language Pashto, directed his team to fall back and find cover. As they did this, he did the opposite. Miller moved toward the enemy, drawing fire toward himself and

U.S. forces found the rugged lands of Afghanistan challenging. All-terrain vehicles and special equipment were adapted to help the military access mountains, deserts, and valleys in search of insurgents.

away from his comrades. He continued to defend himself but was mortally wounded. When American backup arrived, Miller's teammates continued to fight so that they could retrieve his body. Miller, a favorite of many Afghan villagers for his respect for their language and culture, received the Medal of Honor for his ultimate sacrifice.

CAUGHT ON TAPE

In 2006, a National Geographic Channel team became embedded with a group of Green Berets in south central Afghanistan. Media are usually only allowed such access for forty-eight hours at a time, but special permission was given to National Geographic to videotape, record, and travel with the Special Forces for ten days. The small force—about two dozen soldiers—was based in a stronghold called Fire Base Cobra, which oversaw an area about the size of Rhode Island known to have a heavy Taliban presence.

The 2007 documentary that resulted, *Inside the Green Berets*, was a snapshot of the men's twofold mission: to win the confidence of the Afghan people and to fight the Taliban. After months of the Special Forces trying to win the village elders' trust, the elders arrived at the base and declared that they wanted peace. But could the Green Berets trust the elders? The villages were under great pressure to obey Taliban commands, sometimes under punishment of death. The Special Forces hoped their actions would prove to the villages that they meant no harm.

A group of the Green Berets, along with the National Geographic team, traveled a great distance to two of the villages to provide medical care and supplies, such as radios tuned to an American-sanctioned station. Many villagers were malnourished and welcomed the medical sergeant. A second objective, to find an Afghan informant who was reporting American movements to the Taliban, was not as successful. In the pitch-black night, the team finally arrived at the ridge they believed would be the safest spot to rest. However, improvised explosive devices (IEDs) were set up all over the ridge. After clearing seven, the group slowly moved up in their vehicles. Sadly, an eighth IED detonated, killing two soldiers, wounding five others, and injuring several of the documentary crew.

COMMITMENT

The Green Berets are the key force in training and working with Afghan soldiers. The need for Afghan natives to defend themselves and their country from the Taliban is paramount. Special Forces have the unique skills to live among the Afghans, learn their languages and culture, and traverse the hills and mountains to locate insurgents. But are their efforts working? Afghans' loyalties are often divided. Firefights have even broken out between American and Afghan soldiers.

A *USA Today* article reported that Afghan locals are increasingly cooperating with Special Forces. Army Brigadier General Jeffrey Smith, of the

WIKILEAKS

WikiLeaks is an organization that publishes private and secret information provided by anonymous sources. The organization claims the right of the freedom of the press to do so. Some of the stories involve classified information that might otherwise never be released. In 2010, WikiLeaks made public military documents about an alleged black ops Special Forces unit called Task Force 373.

Operating in Afghanistan, Task Force 373 has a "kill or capture list" of more than two thousand terrorists and insurgents, according to the newspaper the *Guardian*. The WikiLeaks reports indicate that the unit was responsible for the friendly-fire deaths of numerous Afghan civilians and Afghan police. Yet this unit's involvement in the incidents is not mentioned in official NATO reports, reinforcing their reputation for black operations. The White House condemned the release of these documents and thousands of other WikiLeaks reports, saying that they put the lives of the soldiers and the outcome of the missions in danger.

Combined Security Transition Command-Afghanistan, said that the Taliban "is not re-emerging" in areas where locals have been fully trained. Former U.S. commander David Petraeus believes that the local defense forces in the thousands of rural villages is the key to defeating the Taliban. The Green Berets will continue to build these forces.

GREEN BERETS INTO THE FUTURE

With insurgencies and terrorist groups at large, it seems likely that the role of the Special Forces and other special operations of the U.S. military will become increasingly invaluable. The Green Berets' military knowledge and diplomatic approach will enable the United States to partner with allies and reduce the number of American soldiers committed to conventional warfare.

A Special Forces soldier trains Afghan National Police to use assault rifles. He belongs to a unit of Green Berets that lives among Afghans in an effort to gain their trust.

Just as the Green Berets evolved out of the large-scale combat of World War II, they continue to evolve in the modern world. One of the newer duties of the Special Forces involves counterproliferation. This means Green Berets find, remove, and disarm weapons of mass destruction, including nuclear, biological, and chemical weapons.

Green Berets are also employed in noncombat duties. Several Green Berets worked with the FBI to translate intercepted documents and conversations that stopped a terrorist attack at the Los Angeles International Airport in 1999. Special Forces continue to train foreign governments to deal with drug warlords and traffickers. They have also instructed African game wardens in counterpoaching techniques to help preserve endangered species. Green Berets act as interpreters in U.S. humanitarian operations and offer disaster relief and health care to people around the world. Until they are called home, the Special Forces will keep striving to achieve their mission, wherever they are needed.

GLOSSARY

ACCLIMATE To adjust in response to a change of environment.

AL QAEDA A Muslim organization dedicated to the elimination of a Western presence in Arab countries and militantly opposed to Western foreign policy.

BEDOUIN A nomadic Arab of the Arabian, Syrian, or North African deserts.

CLANDESTINE Conducted in secrecy.

CLASSIFIED Available only to authorized people for reasons of national security.

DISENFRANCHISED Deprived of a privilege, immunity, or legal right, especially the right to vote.

EMBEDDED Covering something closely.

ENLISTED A member of the U.S. armed forces who is lower in rank than a commissioned or warrant officer.

FRIENDLY FIRE Gunfire coming from your own or your allies' forces, not the enemy, which sometimes causes injury or death.

GENEVA CONVENTION One of a series of agreements concerning the treatment of prisoners of war and of the sick, wounded, and dead in battle first made at Geneva, Switzerland, in 1864 and accepted by most nations.

GUERILLA A member of an irregular paramilitary unit, usually with some political objective, such as the overthrow of a government.

INSURGENCY Uprising against a government.

KURDISH A member of a countryside and agricultural people who inhabit a plateau region in parts of Turkey, Iran, Iraq, Syria, Armenia, and Azerbaijan.

LOGISTICS The management of the details of an operation.

MORTAR A cannon with a short, wide barrel, used for firing shells at a high angle for a short distance.

ORIENTEERING An activity that combines map-reading and running.

PARATROOPERS Troops trained and equipped to parachute from an airplane.

RAPPEL To descend by sliding down a rope.

SEMIAUTOMATIC Able to fire repeatedly but requiring release and another pressure of the trigger for each successive shot.

SNIPER One who shoots at exposed individuals from a usually concealed point of vantage.

TACTIC A method used or a course of action followed in order to achieve an immediate or short-term objective.

TALIBAN A fundamentalist Islamic militia in Afghanistan.

VIET CONG A guerrilla member of the Vietnamese Communist movement.

WARRANT OFFICER An officer ranking above a noncommissioned officer and below a commissioned officer; technical and training expert for combat equipment, vehicles, and other materials.

FOR MORE INFORMATION

160th Special Operations Aviation Regiment (Airborne)
2929 Desert Storm Drive
Fort Bragg, NC 28310
(910) 432-6005
Web site: http://www.soc.mil/160th/160th.html
The 160th's mission is to organize, equip, train, and
employ army special operations aviation forces world-
wide in support of missions.

Canadian Special Operations Forces Command
Department of National Defence
National Defence Headquarters
Major-General George R. Pearkes Building
101 Colonel By Drive
Ottawa, ON K1A 0K2
Canada
(613) 995-2534
Web site: http://www.forces.ca
The special military operations of Canada's motto is *Viam
Inveniemus*, "We will find a way."

U.S. Military Academy
Taylor Hall, Building 600
West Point, NY 10996-1788
(845) 938-2006
Web site: http://www.usma.edu

Graduates of the U.S. Military Academy, also known as West Point, become commissioned officers in the army.

U.S. Special Operations Command (SOCOM)
7701 Tampa Point Boulevard
MacDill Air Force Base, FL 33621
(813) 826-4600
Web site: http://www.socom.mil
This is the official command center of SOCOM, the Special Operations Command. Find links to the army and other branches of the U.S. military through this Web site.

Veterans Affairs Canada
P.O. Box 7700
Charlottetown, PE C1A 8M9
Canada
(888) 996-2242
Web site: http://www.veterans.gc.ca
Learn more about the Canadian forces and the men and women who have served their country.

WEB SITES

Due to the changing nature of Internet links, Rosen Publishing has developed an online list of Web sites related to the subject of this book. This site is updated regularly. Please use this link to access the list:

http://www.rosenlinks.com/ISF/GBER

FOR FURTHER READING

Blehm, Eric. *The Only Thing Worth Dying for: How Eleven Green Berets Forged a New Afghanistan.* New York, NY: Harper, 2010.

Couch, Dick. *Chosen Soldier: The Making of a Special Forces Warrior.* New York, NY: Random House, 2007.

Fredriken, John C. *Fighting Elites: A History of U.S. Special Forces.* Santa Barbara, CA: ABC-CLIO, 2012.

Guardia, Mike. *Shadow Commander: The Epic Story of Donald D. Blackburn: Guerrilla Leader and Special Forces Hero.* Havertown, PA: Casemate, 2011.

Hoe, Alan. *The Quiet Professional: Major Richard J. Meadows of the U.S. Army Special Forces.* Lexington, KY: University Press of Kentucky, 2011.

Maylor, Rob, and Robert Macklin. *Sniper Elite: The World of a Top Special Forces Marksman.* New York, NY: St. Martins Press, 2011.

Moore, Robin, and Michael Lennon. *The Wars of the Green Berets: Amazing Stories from Vietnam to the Present.* New York, NY: Skyhorse Publishing, 2007.

Tucker, David and Christopher J. Lamb. *United States Special Operations Forces.* New York, NY: Columbia University Press, 2007.

Urban, Mark. *Task Force Black: The Explosive True Story of the Secret Special Forces War in Iraq.* New York, NY: St. Martin's Press, 2010.

BIBLIOGRAPHY

CBSNews.com. "Green Berets: The Quiet Professionals." *60 Minutes*. January 28, 2010. Retrieved March 1, 2012 (http://www.cbsnews.com/stories/2010/01/28/60minutes/main6151526.shtml).

Clancy, Tom, Carl Stiner, and Tony Koltz. *Shadow Warriors: Inside the Special Forces*. New York, NY: G. P. Putnam's Sons, 2002.

Clark, Josh. "How the Green Berets Work." How Stuff Works. Retrieved January 28, 2012 (http://science.howstuffworks.com/green-beret1.htm).

Couch, Dick. *Chosen Soldier: The Making of a Special Forces Warrior*. New York, NY: Random House, 2007.

Davies, Nick. "Afghanistan War Logs: Task Force 373—Special Forces Hunting Top Taliban." *Guardian*, July 25, 2010. Retrieved February 29, 2012 (http://www.guardian.co.uk/world/2010/jul/25/task-force-373-secret-afghanistan-taliban).

Dyhouse, Tim. "'Black Ops' Shine in Iraq War." *VFW Magazine*, February 2004. Retrieved February 21, 2012 (http://findarticles.com/p/articles/mi_m0LIY/is_5_91/ai_113304758/?tag=content;col1).

Fantz, Ashley, and Tim Lister. "WikiLeaks Shines Spotlight on Mysterious Task Force 373." CNN.com, July 26, 2010. Retrieved March 1, 2012 (http://afghanistan.blogs.cnn.com/2010/07/26/wikileaks-shines-spotlight-on-mysterious-task-force-373).

Foust, Joshua. "Inside the Green Berets in Afghanistan." *The Registan*, June 5, 2007. Retrieved March 20, 2012 (http://registan.net/index.php/2007/06/05/inside-the-green-berets-in-afghanistan).

Gentile, Carmen. "In Afghanistan, Special Units Do the Dirty Work." *USA Today*, November 10, 2011. Retrieved March 3, 2012 (http://www.usatoday.com/news/world/afghanistan/story/2011-11-09/special-forces-key-in-afghanistan/51145690/1).

Halberstadt, Hans. *War Stories of the Green Berets*. St. Paul, MN: Zenith Press, 2004.

Inside NGC. "Inside the Green Berets." National Geographic. Retrieved March 8, 2012 (http://incubator.nationalgeographic.com/inside_ngc/2007/05/inside-the-green-berets.html).

John F. Kennedy Presidential Library and Museum. "Green Berets." Retrieved January 6, 2012 (http://www.jfklibrary.org/JFK/JFK-in-History/Green-Berets.aspx).

Military Times. "Jarion Halbisengibbs." Retrieved March 5, 2012 (http://militarytimes.com/citations-medals-awards/recipient.php?recipientid=3658).

Obama, Barack. "Presidential Remarks." Army.mil, October 6, 2010. Retrived March 21, 2012 (http://www.army.mil/medalofhonor/miller/remarks.html).

Roeder, Tom. "Carson Green Beret's Feat Earns Awe, Medal." *Gazette*, May 14, 2009. Retrieved January 30, 2012 (http://www.gazette.com/articles/halbisengibbs-54030-lindsay-chaney.html).

Shanker, Thom. "How Green Berets Beat the Odds at an Iraq Alamo." *New York Times*, September

22, 2003. Retrieved March 10, 2012 (http://www.
nytimes.com/2003/09/22/world/the-struggle-for-
iraq-combat-how-green-berets-beat-the-odds-at-
an-iraq-alamo.html?pagewanted=all&src=pm).

Sheftick, Gary. "Army Expanding Its Special
Operations Force." U.S. Army, October 27, 2010.
Retrieved February 17, 2012 (http://www.army.mil/
article/47245/army-expanding-its-special-operations-
force).

Sherwood, Ben. "Lessons in Survival." *Daily
Beast*, February 13, 2009. Retrieved February
14, 2012 (http://www.thedailybeast.com/news-
week/2009/02/13/lessons-in-survival.html).

Special Operations.Com. "U.S. Army Special
Forces." Retrieved March 2, 2012 (http://www
.specialoperations.com/Army/Special_Forces/SF_
Info/Detailed_History.htm).

Stanton, Shelby. *Green Berets at War*. Novato, CA:
Presidio Press, 1985.

U.S. Army. "Special Forces." Retrieved February 6,
2012 (http://www.goarmy.com/special-forces/team-
members.html).

U.S. Army Center of Military History. "Medal of Honor
Recipients." Retrieved February 2, 2012 (http://
www.history.army.mil/html/moh/vietnam-a-l.html).

U.S. Army Special Operations Command. "Special
Forces Creed." Retrieved February 20, 2012
(http://www.soc.mil/usasfc/SF%20Creed.html).

Waller, Douglas C. *Commandos: The Inside Story of
America's Secret Soldiers*. New York, NY: Simon &
Schuster, 1994.

INDEX

ABOUT THE AUTHOR

Therese M. Shea, a former educator, is an author and editor of over one hundred children's nonfiction books, including several on U.S. military branches and American war heroes. A graduate of Providence College, the author holds an M.A. in English education from the State University of New York at Buffalo. She currently resides in Atlanta, Georgia, with her husband, Mark.

PHOTO CREDITS

Cover (inset photos) U.S. Army; cover (flare) © iStockphoto.com/Evgeny Terentev; cover (smoke) © iStockphoto.com/Antagain; cover, interior (crosshairs) © iStockphoto.com/marlanu; p. 5 Mark Wilson/Getty Images; pp. 9, 11, 18, 22, 36, 40–41, 43, 52 © AP Images; pp. 12, 35 photos courtesy of DefenseImagery.mil; p. 19 Lance Cpl. Kyle McNally; p. 25 Keystone/Hulton Archive/Getty Images; p. 28 compdrw/Flickr/Getty Images; p. 29 U.S. Department of Defense; p. 45 Patrick Barth/Getty Images; p. 48 U.S. Navy/Getty Images; interior graphics: © iStockphoto.com/P_Wei (camouflage), © iStockphoto.com/Oleg Zabielin (silhouette), © iStockphoto.com/gary milner (texture).

Designer: Brian Garvey; Editor: Nicholas Croce; Photo Researcher: Marty Levick